The Southern Heritage Survival Manual

More than 125 Ways You Can Defend Southern History, Rights & Values

Ron Holland

Traveller Press • Bridgewater, New Jersey

The Southern Heritage Survival Manual
More than 125 Ways You Can Defend Southern History, Rights, and Values
© 2002 by Ron Holland. All rights reserved.
Published in 2002 by Traveller Press

Traveller Press
PO Box 6577
Bridgewater NJ 08807
www.travellerpress.com

All rights reserved. No part of this publication may be reproduced, stored in a retrieval system, or transmitted in any form or by any means — electronic, mechanical, photocopy, recording, digital, or any other — except for brief quotations in printed reviews, without prior permission of the publisher.

Cover & interior design ©2002 Pneuma Books: Complete Publisher's Services
http://www.pneumadesign.com/books/info.htm
Set in Adobe Caslon 12 / 14.75. Titles set in Caslon Antique with subtitles in Caslon 540 Swash. The content of this book is wholly written by the Author and owned by the Publisher. Opinions and suggestions set forth in this book are not necessarily the opinion or view of Pneuma Books.

First Printing. Printed in the United States of America by ThomsonShore, Dexter MI
10 09 08 07 06 05 04 03 02 01   10 9 8 7 6 5 4 3 2 1

Publisher's Cataloging-in-Publication
(*Provided by Quality Books, Inc.*)

Holland, Ron, 1950-
  The Southern heritage survival manual : more than 125 ways you can defend Southern history, rights and values / by Ron Holland. -- 1st ed.
  p.cm.
  ISBN: 0-9713351-4-1

  1. Southern States--Civilization. 2. Political participation--Southern States.
I. Title.

F216.2.H65 2001   975'.044
                        QBI00-789

*Dedicated to
My Friend,
Compatriot and
Southern Gentleman*:

H.K. Edgerton

*— a True & Tireless
Defender of Dixie*

The Publisher Gratefully Acknowledges the
The Museum of the Confederacy
Richmond, Virginia
for granting permission to use the photo of the
Battleflag of the 38th North Carolina Infantry

Photo by Katherine Wetzel

Visit the Museum at
http://www.moc.org

Table of Contents

Foreword	League of the South	*page vii*
Introduction	...to turn the tide...	*page xi*
Chapter One	Educational Activities to Defend Dixie	*page 1*
Chapter Two	Public Actions & Activities to Defend Dixie	*page 17*
Chapter Three	Private Efforts & Activities to Defend Dixie	*page 25*
Chapter Four	Suggestions for Southern Heritage Defence	*page 35*
Chapter Five	Action Ideas for Southern Activists	*page 45*
Chapter Six	Southern Economic & Financial Actions	*page 51*
Chapter Seven	Political & Lobbying Activities	*page 59*
Chapter Eight	Media and Press Actions	*page 69*
Chapter Nine	Utilise the Internet	*page 75*
Conclusion	Always Be Prepared	*page 85*
Appendices	Organisations, Websites, & Publications	*page 91*

A Foreword from League of the South President Dr. Michael Hill

My friend and compatriot Ron Holland has written a book all patriotic Southerners should read and act upon. Knowledge without subsequent action is worthless.

At the beginning of this millennium, we Southerners find our cultural heritage — and our very liberties — under assault by a dangerous alliance of leftist and liberal groups, who, more often than not, are supported by the central government in Washington, D.C. This leftist alliance seeks to destroy the traditional South and that for which it stands. They began with our flag, but they will not stop until they have destroyed all that it represents, including those of us who stand up against their plans to reconstruct the world according to their corrupt vision.

Why is the traditional South anathema to leftist totalitarians? I believe it is because we traditional Southerners understand that our first allegiance is to God, and to His Christ, and that the state must submit itself to His word and dominion. Leftists wish to make the political state our god and use its power to overawe all who oppose their worldview. This state of affairs has worsened since the South's military defeat in 1865. Lincoln ushered in a centralised state that has gradually become able to define the limits of its own power.

The Old American Republic of the Founders died at Appomattox and was replaced by a nascent American Empire that in the twentieth century slipped the bonds of the constitution and became a tyranny. Today, the current regime (Democrat or Republican, it matters not) is dedicated to advancing a godless multiculturalism that is diametrically opposed to the values and mores of Western Christian civilisation. Indeed, the prime enemy of modern leftist hegemony is the remnant of Christian civilisation that refuses to give its sanction to the suicidal policies and practices of the multiculturalists. And nowhere is that remnant more in evidence than in the American South.

It is well that increasing numbers of Southerners and other Americans are beginning to understand the enemy's agenda and what it means for the future of the South in particular and of Western civilisation in general. It is men such as Ron Holland who will show them how to translate their often unproductive anger into productive action in defence of our Southern civilisation. Ron's man-

Foreword : League of the South

ual is a guidebook for those who wish to do more than just talk about defending their birthright.

This book is a valuable addition to the growing body of Southern Nationalist literature. When, God willing, our independence is a reality, no small measure of credit will be due to honourable, courageous, and perceptive men like my friend and fellow League of the South member, Ron Holland.

Dr. Michael Hill
President
The League of the South

Introduction

...to turn the tide...

In recent years the heritage, history, and symbols of Dixie have been under an unrelenting attack by the political, media, and financial establishments of the United States. The South's crime in the eyes of the Washington politicians and the politically correct crowd is simply that we once dared to resist the centralisation of governmental power in Washington, D.C. (and nearly succeeded). The proud and gallant defence of our homes, families, and liberty during Abraham Lincoln's unconstitutional war of invasion against the Confederate States of America shall never be forgotten. More than 250,000 brave Confederates — white, black, Latino, and American Indian — gave their lives in that epic struggle for independence and resistance to tyranny.

Dixie ultimately lost her independence, but the United States lost something as well: the original constitutional republic established by the Founding Fathers. It was subverted by the illegal acts of the centralised federal government — behaviour that continues to this day to infringe upon state sovereignty and individual rights at home and upon foreign nations abroad.

I wrote *The Southern Heritage Survival Manual* to educate Southern people in the ways to use political action, media public relations, and the modern technology of the Internet, to turn the tide against those who would rewrite or erase our history, tear down our monuments, and outlaw the celebration of Southern history, symbols, and culture. Inside these pages I provide several suggestions and recommend many resources to assist the average Southerner (and those who sympathise with our Cause) in their quest to honorouably and democratically defend our heritage, rights, and way of life. Refer to the appendices for contact information for the many organizations, publications, and websites mentioned throughout the manual.

My desire is that this book should serve as a warning to both major political parties of the Establishment that dominate political action and the electoral process in this country today. They should either leave our Southern symbols, heritage, and rights alone or we may just decide that we have had enough.

I predict that the twenty-first century will be one of political devolution. The next few years will be a time

Introduction : ...to turn the tide...

of independence and democratic secession movements throughout the world. The United States are certainly not immune to this; every attack upon our Confederate flags, our monuments, and our right to celebrate our history serves no other purpose than to add fuel to the fire of Southern nationalism and independence. Like our Confederate ancestors, those of us in Dixie wish for nothing more than to be left alone — or we may just decide to leave.

Would leaving really be such a bad thing? After all, where would the United States be without Dixie's soldiers in their armed forces, which are now based in over one hundred nations around the globe? Or without the tax receipts from our growing economy here in the Sun Belt? How long could the United States remain competitive against an independent Dixie with low taxes and tariffs, financial privacy, and a free market just south of its border? I think the answers are self-evident.

I must, however, make one point clear; the ideas and actions mentioned in this book are in no way meant to be construed to call for or advocate unlawful or subversive actions. I do not support the overthrow of the United States Government nor violent or illegal actions against it. Rather, Dixie's interests are best achieved through education, lobbying, and the democratic process in a manner consistent with our Southern beliefs and traditions: the democratic and honourable principles of law and order.

~ *R.H.* ~

Chapter One

Educational Activities to Defend Dixie

Educate yourself in the subjects of liberty and Southern heritage. You must first grasp the ideas and be well-versed in the subject matter yourself if you intend to persuade others to support Southern heritage and values. This chapter contains lists of highly recommended sources for your search. Remember that these should only serve as a genesis for your self-education — never cease in your quest for knowledge.

1 *Subscribe to Pro-South Publications*
Several available periodicals are well worth the subscription price. These magazines and newsletters pro-

vide insightful articles written by Southern intellectuals and others who sympathise with our Cause. The great thing about such publications is that after you have finished reading them, you can lend them to a friend or simply leave them for others to read (in a doctor's office, for example). Refer to Appendix C for some recommended publications.

1 *Build a Personal Library of Freedom and Pro-South Books*
Here are some books I highly recommend:

- Adams, Charles—
  When In the Course of Human Events
  (Lanham, Md.: Rowman & Littlefield Publishing Group, 2000).
  Adams argues for the legality of secession and the true cause of the War for Southern Independence — oppressive tariffs that were unfair to the South.

- Applebome, Peter—
  Dixie Rising
  (New York: Times Books, 1996).
  The author makes his case that the South has recently taken the lead in shaping the American political and cultural landscape.

- Bledsoe, Albert Taylor—
  Is Davis A Traitor?
  (Richmond, Va.: The Hermitage Press, 1907).
  A look at secession philosophy and constitutionality prior to the advent of war in 1861.

Educational Activities to Defend Dixie

- Bradford, M. E. —
  A Better Guide Than Reason
  (Somerset, N.J.: Transaction Publishers, 1994).
  > An examination of the Federalists and their anti-Federalist counterparts in the founding of the Union.

- Browne, Harry—
  How I Found Freedom In an Unfree World
  (New York: Macmillan, 1973).
  > Advice on how to take control of your life and fight against that which restricts your freedom from former Libertarian Party presidential candidate.

- Dabney, R. L.—
  Discussions
  (London: Banner of Truth Trust, 1982).
  > Expositions by a minister who once served as chief of staff to Stonewall Jackson.

- Davis, Jefferson—
  The Rise and Fall of the Confederate Government
  (New York: T. Yoseloff, 1958).
  > An invaluable resource written by the chief executive of the Confederate States of America.

- Davis, William C.—
  A Government of Our Own: The Making of the Confederacy
  (New York: Free Press, 1994).
  > A well-researched look at the major players dur-

ing the establishment of the Confederate government in Montgomery.

- Fischer, David Hackett—
The Great Wave: Price Revolutions and the Rhythm of History
(Oxford: Oxford University Press, 2000).
Brandeis University professor explains the effects of economic policy upon historical events.

- Gordon, David, ed.—
Secession, State and Liberty
(Somerset, N.J.: Transaction Publishers, 1998).
A thorough examination of secession, past and "future."

- Grissom, Michael Andrew—
Southern By the Grace of God
(Gretna, La.: Pelican Publishing Company, 1988).
A book that celebrates Southern traditions and culture, it is widely credited with initiating the recent resurgence of Southern nationalism.

- Harwell, Richard B.—
The Confederate Reader: How the South Saw the War
(Mineola, N.Y.: Dover Publications, Inc., 1989).
A selection of contemporary writings, battle reports, and articles that paints a picture of Southern motivations and beliefs during the War for Southern Independence.

- Hummel, Jeffrey Rogers—
*Emancipating Slaves, Enslaving Free Men:
A History of the American Civil War*
(Chicago: Open Court Publishing Co., 1996).
> Hummel examines the causes of a war he feels was not inevitable and the centralisation of government power in Washington, D.C. that resulted.

- Kennedy, James Ronald and Walter D. Kennedy—
The South Was Right!
(Gretna, La.: Pelican Publishing Company, 1994).
> The bible for the modern Southern nationalist. The Kennedy brothers make the case for the Lost Cause and debunk the "Yankee Myth" of history.

- ———

  Was Jefferson Davis Right?
  (Gretna, La.: Pelican Publishing Company, 1998).
  > A powerful apologetic for the Confederates' (accurate) view of states' rights and secession. The authors give Davis what the U.S. government never did — a fair trial.

- ———

  *Why Not Freedom?
  America's Revolt Against Big Government*
  (Gretna, La.: Pelican Publishing Company, 1995).
  > The authors discuss the United States' transition from a union of sovereign states to a centralised behemoth government administered by bureaucrats concerned only with their own well-being at

the expense of personal liberties (supposedly) guaranteed by the Constitution.

- Locke, John—
  Second Treatise on Government
  (Indianapolis, Ind.: Hackett Publishing Co., 1980).
    The touchstone for traditional American political thought. Locke's views on limited government, property rights, and popular sovereignty shaped the actions of the Founding Fathers and served as the genesis for the original American Republic.

- Lytle, Andrew—
  Why the South Will Survive: Fifteen Southerners Look at Their Region a Half Century After "I'll Take My Stand"
  (Athens, Ga.: University of Georgia Press, 1983).
    A follow-up to the Fugitive Agrarians.

- McDonald, Forrest—
  States' Rights and the Union: Imperium in Imperio, 1776-1876
  (Lawrence, Kans.: University Press of Kansas, 2000).
    McDonald examines the increasingly adversarial relationship between the states and the federal government through "Reconstruction."

- Masters, Edgar Lee—
  Lincoln the Man
  (New York: Dodd, Mead & Company, 1931).
    Masters demolishes the Lincoln myth.

Educational Activities to Defend Dixie

- Mises, Ludwig von—
  Human Action: A Treatise on Economics
  (New Haven, Conn.: Yale University Press, 1949).
  > The author remains unsurpassed among advocates of a free-market economy.

- Naylor, Thomas and William H. Willimon—
  Downsizing the USA
  (Grand Rapids, Mich.: Wm. B. Eerdmans Publishing Co., 1997).
  > The authors argue for the devolution and decentralisation of American society.

- Rable, George C.—
  The Confederate Republic: A Revolution Against Politics
  (Chapel Hill, N.C.: University of North Carolina Press, 1994).
  > Rable examines the tension between the Confederacy's attempts to re-establish a republic worthy of the Founding Fathers and the realities of partisan politics.

- Stephens, Alexander H.—
  Constitutional View of the Late War Between the States: Its Causes, Character, and Results
  (Philadelphia: National Publishing Company, 1868-1870).
  > The Vice President of the Confederate States of America defends the secession acts of the Southern states in light of the U.S. Constitution.

- Thomas, Emory M.—
  Confederate Nation: 1861-1865
  (New York: Harper & Row, 1979).
  A concise but comprehensive account of the Southern war effort.

- Thornton, R. Gordon.—
  The Southern Nation and the New Rise of the Old South
  (Gretna, La.: Pelican Publishing Company, 2000).
  The author decries the years of subjugation (and Yankee occupation) endured by the South and offers solutions for the reassertion of Dixie's independence.

3 *Visit Southern Battlefields and Heritage Sites*

Nothing quite captures the spirit of our forefathers' sacrifices like standing on the ground where the struggle occurred. But Southern history covers far more than the Virginia battlefields. The bravery exhibited by the gallant men of Pickett's division really hits home when you gaze across the open fields of Gettysburg upon which they marched. Make sure you visit Fort Sumter and other landmarks in Charleston, South Carolina; the Confederate White House in Richmond; the Alabama Capitol and First White House of the Confederacy in Montgomery; Shiloh Battlefield in Tennessee; Vicksburg, Mississippi; and other prominent landmarks. The Fortress Dixie website provides a list of many Southern battlefield sites.

Remember, the more you know about the gallant struggles for the Constitution and Southern Indepen-

Educational Activities to Defend Dixie

dence, the better you can defend our proud Southern history and heritage.

4 *Write a Booklet or Pamphlet on Some Aspect of the Southern Experience*
Consider writing and publishing an informational booklet about the War for Southern Independence in your local area for distribution to interested persons, heritage groups, and schools. This will help you to discover new Confederate friends, support the Cause, and improve your knowledge of local Southern history. I urge you to read the League of the South booklet *Confederate Columbia* as an example. Your pamphlet can range from a scholarly publication of some length to a photocopied local history of only a few pages. When writing a booklet, always be sure to list the names and address of appropriate Southern organisations and websites, including Fortress Dixie.

5 *Get Your Children Out of Public Schools when Necessary*
Some public schools are good and some are not; some teachers present a fair representation of the War for Southern Independence and others do not. I understand that this suggestion is an individual choice; I have one child in an excellent public school and two in private schools. However, with most public and private schools it is a good idea to supplement the Northern bias in educational materials with a few good books at home that promote the truth about the war and the South.

6 *Consider a Private Christian School*
The same warnings about public schools can be made for

Christian private schools as can for public schools. Again, you have to make the best decision for your children. It is also important that you supplement the school study and reading materials with pro-South books appropriate for the age and maturity level of your child.

7. *Homeschooling Options*
The public (or government) schools are often little more than anti-Southern, anti-Christian propaganda mills. Although homeschooling is not an option for many parents because of economic constraints, you should give it serious consideration. Make this sacrifice for your children.

There are numerous homeschool resources and organisations from which parents can draw ideas and support in educating their children in accordance with Southern, Christian values. A cursory search on the Internet or at your public library should assist you in getting the help you need to decide whether homeschooling is right for you and your children.

A good place to start is Jon's Homeschool Resource Page on the Internet at www.midnightbeach.com/hs/. This site answers many of the frequently asked questions about homeschooling and provides links to several other websites and books on the subject.

8. *Start a Monthly Southern Reading Club*
Make new friends and educate yourself and your family about topics of interest. Get together to discuss books on Southern history, literature, or politics. Other areas of reading and discussion could include the Constitution, theology, or current events.

Educational Activities to Defend Dixie

9 *Contribute Pro-South Books to Your Municipal and School Library*
Donate pro-South books such as *The South Was Right!* or *When in the Course of Human Events* to your local library. Consider inviting a local newspaper photographer or television camera crew to be there when you make the presentation. This makes a good local story, especially in small towns. If the media representatives fail to appear, have someone take a photograph and send it to the local newspaper with a short press release. Note that many "local" newspapers are actually owned by distant, liberal global publishing empires, so if they fail to run your story, look into it. Find out if anti-Southern bias played a part in the rejection and make that a story.

10 *Turn No Press Coverage into Big Press Coverage*
If the local paper refuses to report on your Southern news event, consider picketing the newspaper business with a sign such as, "Newspaper Against Local Southern History and Heritage." That may attract the newspaper coverage you were seeking, plus local radio and television coverage. The Establishment Media prefer to ignore our events, but if they are faced with negative publicity, that could generate a backlash of resentment against their actions and force them to run the story in order to stop the bad publicity.

11 *Purchase Gift Subscriptions to Pro-South Magazines for Your City and School Libraries*
Ask if you can purchase a gift magazine subscription for a friend, family member, political or business leader, or local library. Consider gift subscriptions to pro-South-

ern publications such as *The Edgefield Journal*, *Southern Partisan*, or *Southern Events*.

12 *Purchase a Conventional "Civil War" Magazine Subscription for the Library if They Are Reluctant to Agree to Southern Publications*
Consider a politically correct subscription to *Civil War Times Illustrated* or *America's Civil War*. Although it is often difficult to find, the truth about the South's position still comes through the politically correct propaganda required by many magazine publishers.

13 *Bring Your Family and Friends to an LOS Hedge School Event*
Consider attending the LOS Summer School and / or Hedge School seminar classes offered at various times and locations throughout the South. Refer to the LOS website for more details on the Hedge Schools and to see the schedule for future events. You may also want to refer to The Dixie Calendar (available on the Internet) for more information on that mentioned above and more than two hundred other scheduled events sponsored by the SCV, LOS, reenactment groups, and historical organisations.

14 *Sponsor an LOS Hedge School in Your Community*
Help others learn more about Southern history, heritage, and culture through the LOS Hedge School Program. If you are interested in organising a Hedge School Seminar in your area, please contact:
Dr. Donald Livingston, Director,

Educational Activities to Defend Dixie

League of the South Institute
for the Study of Southern Culture and History,
478 Burlington Road
Atlanta, Georgia 30307
office telephone and fax: (404) 377-0484.

15 *Attend Schools, Conferences, and Seminars on Important Freedom Topics*
For seminars on the free market, the Constitution, secession, and freedom-related topics, review the excellent seminar schedule sponsored by the Ludwig von Mises Institute. Other institutions sponsoring free market seminars are the Foundation For Economic Education, Cato Institute, Future of Freedom Foundation, and the Heritage Foundation. For a complete list of conservative and free market institutes and foundations, refer to the Austrian and Free Market Bookstore.

16 *Attend Local, State, and National Conventions of Pro-South Organisations*
The Sons of Confederate Veterans, League of the South, United Daughters of the Confederacy, and the Southern Party, among others, have interesting and educational state and national conferences. For a current list of Southern events, conferences, schools, and re-enactments, refer to *The Dixie Calendar*.

17 *Buy Conference Audiotapes and Videotapes if You Cannot Attend Events*
If you cannot attend the conferences of your choice, consider ordering the tapes, transcripts, and video record-

ings from the organisations sponsoring the event(s). It is the next best thing to being there!

18 *Buy Time on a Local Radio Station and Spread the Message*
Many talk and religious radio stations have time available outside of their prime hours. Consider purchasing audio cassettes from the Apologia Book Shoppe or the LOS for broadcast.

19 *Buy and Distribute Southern Audiotapes and Videotapes*
Consider the *History and Literature of the South* lecture tape series sponsored by the League of the South Institute for the Study of Southern History and Culture or the *Southern Independence Day* video of the march and speeches in Montgomery, Alabama. Also consider ordering the many Southern heritage videos from the H. K. Edgerton Book and Video Store, including *From the Dome to the Ground — Columbia, SC July 1, 2000* (an exclusive interview with H. K. Edgerton) and *Southern Heritage 2000 and The Confederate Flag Controversy.*

20 *Promote a Confederate Mascot for Your Local School Sports Team*
Do not expect success in this type of effort until we are stronger, but just going on the offensive with publicity and petitions will remind the local PC crowd that we will not give up. This, in turn, could relieve some pressure from their offensives in other heritage battles. This is a cultural war against Dixie. Remember, in all situations we must stop fighting defensively and go on the offensive — even if we lose most of the battles.

Educational Activities to Defend Dixie

<u>21</u> *Are You Uncomfortable with Confederate Symbols?*
Although I personally believe that we must stand behind our hallowed symbols, some of our compatriots believe that we should downplay the Confederate flag because there are those who constantly mention the instances in which racists and hate groups have stolen our Southern symbols and used them for nefarious purposes. If you agree with this position for marketing or promotional reasons, then get involved with and help promote Jim Langcuster's Home Rule for Dixie website. Jim downplays historical Confederate symbolism and advocates the social and cultural, rather than political, secession of the South. I want more people to defend Dixie, so I continue to support Jim's approach (and many others), so long as it means bringing more compatriots into our ranks.

Chapter Two

Public Actions & Activities to Defend Dixie

Although self-improvement and education in Southern issues is important, it pales in comparison to those actions we must take to win others to our side. In addition, there are scores of people who may already agree with our positions but feel they are in a minority. Publicly announcing our love of Dixie will demonstrate to others that there are many like-minded people around, thus encouraging them to join the Movement.

22 *Fly the Third National Flag at Your Home and Business*
Show the colours in your front yard or business (if self-employed). We cannot expect state politicians in Atlanta,

Columbia, Tallahassee, or Jackson to take the heat by defending our flag and heritage if we are not willing to do so ourselves. It is, of course, your choice whether to fly the Confederate Battle flag or the Third National flag. For those of you in neighbourhoods or professions that require a measure of moderation and caution in promoting Dixie, consider the First National flag or Bonnie Blue as the symbol of your Southern heritage. One of the best sources of Southern flags is the Ruffin Flag Company.

One of the best examples to follow is that of Maurice Bessinger, owner of Maurice's BBQ in South Carolina. Although it has cost him in bad press and lost revenues (Wal-Mart ceased carrying his barbecue sauce), Maurice continues to fly a Confederate Battle flag, along with the state flag, at every one of his restaurants.

23 *Display a Pro-South Sign*
Consider inscribing pro-South slogans on your personal property or on the sides and/ or roofs of barns, similar to the old "Visit Rock City" advertisements. One appropriate slogan would be "Southern Independence Now!" followed by the Battle flag logo and a toll-free number and website URL for the LOS state or local chapter.

Another suggestion would be to promote the Sons of Confederate Veterans with the phrase "Southern Heritage, Not Hate" followed by the SCV logo, toll-free number, and website URL.

24 *Rent a Billboard or Erect a Flag Display*
If your property borders a well-travelled highway or an

Public Actions & Activities to Defend Dixie

interstate, consider working with a local LOS, SCV, or Southern Party organisation to put up a billboard and/or Confederate flagpole. This is especially important for North to South interstate highways coming into Dixie, such as I-95. Imagine if there were multiple billboards and Confederate flags flying in each southern state through which I-95 passes as the New Yorkers and others drive down to their winter homes. We need to promote the idea that Dixie is a distinct region.

The Southern Party of Georgia sponsored a 12 foot by 24 foot billboard that greets visitors as they travel down Highway 215. What a great way to say, "Howdy!" For additional information on how you can help sponsor a billboard for a rather inexpensive cost, contact the SCV camp or chapter in your area.

25 *Buy Land Next to a Highway or Interstate*
Property is usually very expensive near intersections and in commercial areas but raw land out in the rural countryside adjacent to an interstate (and far away from an exit) is often reasonably priced. If you plan to invest in land or if you have some extra money you want to put to work for profits and Dixie, look at land with an eye toward the view from the highway. Imagine if Southerners all across the South would put up flagpoles flying the sacred banners of Dixie!

26 *Promote a Pro-South Speaker at Meetings and Events*
Invite Southern heritage and Southern independence speakers to local church, heritage, and civic group meetings. (If you work for the federal government you should beware whom you invite.) There is a wide range of

speakers promoting Southern heritage (such as H. K. Edgerton) and independence who would be appropriate for many meetings and events. Contact the LOS, SCV, and other pro-Southern organisations for more details or refer to the Southern Caucus website's list of recommended speakers.

27 *Become a Public Speaker for Dixie*
The Southern Movement always needs good, qualified speakers. Just make sure you have carefully studied your topic before you commit to a public engagement. You never know who will be on hand to watch, so I strongly suggest that you write the text of your speech out beforehand. The Southern Caucus List of Recommended Speakers is always looking for new speakers to add to our extensive list of Southern history, heritage defence, and independence speakers. Begin speaking at your local SCV or other organisation meetings and continue from there.

28 *Go On the Flag Offensive for Dixie*
Promote Dixie on your own. Drive to work or school with a Confederate Battle flag on your car antenna or from the bed of your pickup truck. Wear a Confederate flag jacket through the Atlanta Airport (as my wife has) or another crowded public place. As a warning, be wise; choose your locations carefully and do not provoke an incident that might put you or others at risk. America has become a violent society. Be aware that there are many dangers in this type of action. Consider Confederate martyr Michael Westerman who was shot and killed for no

Public Actions & Activities to Defend Dixie

other reason than that he displayed a Confederate flag on his truck!

29 Celebrate Southern Heritage, History, and Cultural Events

Attend and participate in battle reenactments, living history exhibits, and Southern heritage events. These events are only successful if people are there to participate in and enjoy them. Be aware that battle re-enacting requires a great deal of dedication and pecuniary resources, so do your research before you commit.

30 Always Ask the Band to Play Dixie (Even Up in Boston!)

If you are at an event where the band is taking requests, you should always ask them to play "Dixie." My business partner did this up in Boston of all places and it worked. He tipped the band at the historic Black Rose Irish Bar in Boston twenty dollars and said, "I'll bet you're too politically correct to play 'Dixie' up here in Boston." Much to his surprise (and delight) the band played it. While about sixty percent of the patrons were liberal Yankees who sat there stone-faced, roughly forty percent of them whooped and cheered and even offered an occasional rebel yell. Some Southerners even were calling out the names of their native states while my wife, standing on top of a table, led the audience in a stirring rendition of our Southern anthem. If this can happen in Boston it can happen anywhere. Czech playwright (and later president of the Czech Republic) Vaclav Havel once noted that one of the things the Communist oppressors feared was a spontaneous outpouring of dissent. We need more politically incorrect spontaneity in these PC times.

31 *Put Together a Southern Band*
Bring together like-minded musicians to form a band. Southerners are highly motivated by good, patriotic music (for exmaple, "Dixie," and "The Bonnie Blue Flag," etc.). Others, like myself, are really into Southern Rock and songs like "Sweet Home Alabama" and "When It All Goes South..." The best way to ensure that the right kind of music is played is to play it yourself.

32 *Book a Confederate Band*
For your next public gathering, ball, or re-enactment event, hire a group like the Un-Reconstructed Band. There is a myriad of bands available that specialise in traditional Celtic and Southern music — all you have to do is find them.

If you cannot afford to hire a live band (or if you do not have the space available) you can do the next best thing — play Southern music on your stereo. Turn up your Southern pride by blasting Lynyrd Skynyrd, the Allman Brothers, or the Marshall Tucker Band through your speakers.

33 *Wear a Confederate Flag Shirt to School or Work*
"Tolerance" seems to be a one way street these days, so be prepared to lose your job or to be sent home from school. My suggestion (if you are in school) is to get your parents' permission first, then familiarise yourself with your rights. Consider talking with Kirk Lyons at the SLRC before provoking a fight. Another valuable resource is the SLRC's *Advice on Southern Civil Rights for Parents and Activists*.

34 *Promote Dixie Everywhere*

I would never advocate that you write pro-South slogans on currency (even though that offensive image of Abraham Lincoln is on every five dollar bill) or that you deface public property (it is, after all, against the law to do either). However, private property is a different matter. On a recent visit to Padania, the aspiring nation in northern Italy, I noticed pro-independence graffiti on every vacant house, wall, and barn. It provided a very effective message — one that could easily be emulated here.

Chapter Three

Private Efforts & Actions to Defend Dixie

Many of us, for whatever reason, prefer private, less controversial ways to express our support for Southern rights and heritage. This is understandable in today's anti-Southern climate. People should only participate in those methods best suited to their situation or disposition. The important thing is that you do *something*. This chapter includes some less controversial ways to convey our Southern message.

35. *Place a Marker at the Grave of Your Confederate Ancestor*
Show your respect for your ancestor's sacrifice by requesting a Standard Application for Government Headstone or Marker from the United States Department of

Veterans Affairs. (This idea is courtesy of Major Egbert A. Ross of SCV Camp #1423 in Charlotte, North Carolina.)

36 *Buy and Display Southern Art and Prints*
I have had a picture of General Robert E. Lee in my office for years, which often turns out to be the topic of conversation with visitors. Consider displaying similar artwork at your home, office, or place of business. There are numerous Internet and "brick-and-mortar" stores offering "Civil War" art (their term not mine). Review the extensive list of Southern products and heritage businesses listed on Fortress Dixie for samples of Southern art and prints available.

37 *Play Southern Music*
Consider playing Southern music by bands such as the Un-Reconstructed Band and Bobby Horton in your home, car, and place of business. Again, who can listen to "Dixie" or "The Bonnie Blue Flag" and not feel the fighting spirit of Dixie? Remember, our Southern music is just as important as our symbols. Refer to the selection of Southern music at Dixie General Store.

38 *Create Time for a Daily Personal Study of the South*
Find time each day to study our Southern heritage and ponder how you can best help defend Dixie. Sit under a shade tree in the park with a book about Stonewall Jackson or recline on the couch with a Southern magazine.

39 *Become a Dixie Advocate*
Advocate Dixie among your friends, clubs, church, and

social activities. Promote the South and our heritage in your daily conversations with friends and associates. Recommend specific books, websites, and publications that advance the Cause. Be low-key and tactful, and respect those with differing opinions. You will attract more flies with honey than you will with vinegar.

40 *Promote Our Minority Status*
Washington would like to ignore the fact that the Confederate States of America existed as an independent, sovereign nation for four years. Those of the South who have ancestors who lived in the Confederacy during the years from 1861 to 1865 are descendants of Confederate-Americans. Therefore, they are a national origin group that should be recognised by the courts and the federal government as having the same rights, privileges, and legal recourse concerning discrimination as any other valid group. Kirk Lyons, head of the SLRC, is now carrying our battle for minority status through the federal court system, where it will eventually be brought before the United States Supreme Court. I send this fine organisation money each and every month; I hope you will also help support this Southern civil rights organisation.

41 *Be a Good Steward of Your Property*
God commands us to practise good stewardship over the gifts with which He has blessed us. Besides, it makes a good impression on the rest of the community if we do so. We all know the "white trash" stereotype with which the Establishment Press has saddled rural Southerners, so we should not conform to their conventions and lend credence to their aspersions. (So keep your yard clean!)

42 Be on the Lookout for Moles, Informants, and Agent Provocateurs

Be aware that those opposed to Dixie often do not fight fair or deal honestly with her defenders. We are considered a threat to their livelihood, jobs, social position, or way of life. We are engaged in a culture war. Our opponents will plant people in the Movement to disrupt organisations, cause internal dissent and disorder, and pass privileged information to the Political Establishment.

Also remember that there will be short-term plants among us tasked specifically with causing embarrassment for the Southern Movement, conforming to negative stereotypes for the benefit of the media. They will also make offensive comments to the press during interviews and Southern events. Keep on the lookout for these undercover agents of the Political Establishment.

Moles are usually easy to detect. If someone constantly creates disruption and infighting among the Southern Movement then they are part of the problem and not the solution. However, be prudent when making accusations; we never want to accuse someone falsely.

43 Report Any Suggestions of Improper, Imprudent, or Illegal Behaviour to Compatriots

The opposition will sometimes attempt to lead those involved in the Southern Movement into committing acts that could embarrass the honourable people of the South. Remember, in order to defend Southern heritage and advance the cause of self-determination for the people of Dixie, we must work within the established democratic political system.

Therefore, we must banish the few outside, evil purveyors of racial hatred and prejudice, as well as those from within the Southern Movement, that would fracture or divide the Movement because they are misguided or professional agent provocateurs. If you discover this sort of behaviour you should immediately contact the leaders of your organisation.

44 *Make Your Vehicle a Mobile Advertisement for Dixie*
I am not suggesting that you plaster your car or truck with every conservative or pro-South bumper sticker you can get your hands on. However, if it is legal in your state, consider putting a Southern-oriented license plate on the front of your vehicle. Many of the Southern heritage businesses listed in the Fortress Dixie Heritage Products Directory have an excellent selection from which to choose. By placing the First or Third National flags of the Confederate States, the Confederate Battle flag, or the Bonnie Blue flag on your vehicle, every car you meet on the highway will see that you stand for Dixie.

You may also want to place a bumper sticker on the rear of your car that promotes your favourite Southern organisation or proclaims your pride in your Southern heritage. (One of my favourites is an oversized decal reading, "Don't Blame Me, I Voted For Jeff Davis.")

Finally, if you are a member of a Southern heritage organisation, such as the SCV, that has an organisation license plate, do your duty by purchasing one for each of your vehicles.

45 *Engage In Private, "Low-key" Protests*
Personally, I rebel (pun intended) against the patriotic songs of the United States. When songs that are polit-

ically offensive to me and Dixie, such as "The Battle Hymn of the Republic," are sung during church or sporting events, I simply stand quietly as others sing. I do the same when the Pledge of Allegiance is recited; there is no reason to make an issue of it and we should not make those around us feel uncomfortable. Nevertheless, we should not participate in activities that offend us. It is a sad state of affairs in the United States of America when we have to stand for the national anthem but are prohibited from praying publicly before an event.

As a further expression of quiet protest, I have consistently declined to teach Sunday school lessons on American patriotism or to participate in any voluntary activity that aids and abets the interests of the Washington government. Again, I do not make a big issue of it; I simply suggest that there are others who could do a better job than I.

46 *Pay Money to Fly a Confederate Banner*
Recently, I had the opportunity to attend an exciting football game pitting Clemson against Georgia Tech. During the game, a plane circled above the stadium pulling a banner that pictured a Confederate flag and the words "Go Tigers." Imagine a plane circulating above a large sporting event while pulling a Confederate flag and maybe a short statement like "Heritage, Not Hate" or "Southern Independence Now!" The banner at Clemson alone reached more than 50,000 people for a relatively low cost.

47 *Mail Your Letters with Confederate "Stamps"*
Order replicas of Confederate states postage stamps; the

CSA Label Company carries a wonderful selection that have been beautifully duplicated on return address mailing labels. These stamps provide a great way to promote the Cause and frustrate the U.S. Postal Service employees who are dependent on their cushy, high-paying jobs with the federal government. Remember, for slow mail, use the U.S. Postal Service headquartered in Washington, D.C. If it has to get there quickly, use Dixie's own Federal Express, which is located in Memphis, Tennessee.

48 *Place a Confederate Message on All of Your Outgoing Envelopes*
A few years ago I would have recommended that you go down to your local office supply store and buy an ink stamp pad with your favourite Confederate slogan to stamp your outgoing envelopes. Today, however, you can print the Southern statement of your choice directly onto your envelopes with your home computer. Consider "Heritage, Not Hate" or the name and website address of your preferred Southern organisation.

49 *Consider Adding "CSA" After the ZIP (Yankee Occupation) Code of Your Return Address*
This is a great way to generate some thinking on the part of federal postal employees and those receiving the mail. If combined with a slogan and website address of your favourite Southern heritage organisation, the person opening the mail will have the opportunity to learn more about our message. My office once promoted an investment conference in a Confederate publication; those who received our mail immediately noticed the "CSA" and came to me with questions.

50 *Speak and Write in the Traditional Southern Manner*

Southerners can be immediately recognised by our unique accent and colloquialisms. Unfortunately, our lovely Southern dialect has become diluted by the influence of Yankee-dominated television. In addition, we have been shamed into believing that our slow Southern drawl makes us sound uneducated or ignorant and that we should mask it with the more generic, Midwest form of speech. However, the Southern dialect is beautiful and we should embrace it. In that vein, wear your native tongue as a badge of honour; say "howdy" rather than "hello" and, of course, refer to more than one person as "y'all." If you are not ashamed to be a Southerner, you should not be ashamed to sound like one.

You may also have noticed the unusual spellings of several words employed in this work. However, this is the traditional spelling scheme used by our Southern ancestors. R. Gordon Thornton does a tremendous job in his book *The Southern Nation and the New Rise of the Old South* explaining the English origins of our Southern language and the Yankee campaign to stamp it out and replace it with an antiseptic, Northern version of spelling and grammar. Familiarise yourself with the traditional, English rules of spelling. This is one of the easiest (and most often used) manners in which we can display our Southern heritage.

In addition, reject the propagandised vocabulary foisted upon us by the Yankee media. Refer to the late struggle by what it was — the War for Southern Independence. The term *Civil War* is not only inaccurate, (such a conflict is defined as a struggle between peoples of one nation to control that nation's government), it is meant to cast our Southern ancestors as traitors. Correct others when they refer to the "Civil War." Send a letter or an e-mail to the editor of your local newspaper when they use the term in a story; if we allow them to do so unchecked, we are lending tacit credence to their argument that the secession of the Southern states was, in fact, illegal and they therefore were deserving of the invasion by the Blue Hoard.

51 *Chivalry Is Not Dead*
Southerners can be recognised by our inherent good manners. Raise your children to address their elders by "sir" and "ma'am." Demand that they ask for things politely and show their gratitude by saying "thank you." And by all means, tell someone "God bless you!" when they sneeze!

Try speaking to total strangers in public by saying "howdy" or just asking how they are doing. (At the very least, we can afford someone a nod and a smile as we pass along the street.)

Southern gentlemen should respect the fairer sex by opening doors for them, pulling out their chairs when they are seated, rising when a lady enters the room, and giving up their seats on a crowded bus, and so forth. We know what good manners are, so let us employ them. We do not want to mirror those in Yankee society, who show no deference, kindness, or respect for anyone but themselves.

Chapter Four

Suggestions for Southern Heritage Defence

In addition to individual actions, it is important to consider banding together with other like-minded Southerners (and those sympathetic to our Cause) to further the interests of Dixie. While the obvious advantage is that there is strength in numbers, one should not overlook the positive fringe benefits to be gained through fellowship and camaraderie. There is no reason why we should not be able to make friends while defending Southern values.

52 *Join Interstate Southern Patriotic Organisations*
Become a part of the interstate Southern organisations best suited to your politics, heritage ideas, and person-

al interests. Your dues and views can help defend our Southern heritage and promote a free Dixie. Become active and involved to ensure more of these organisations promote the right of secession and regional autonomy as a check against the continuing centralisation of government power.

There are also many state Southern political parties now organising throughout the South. The Fortress Dixie website provides links to several of these organisations.

53 *Join a Local Southern Organisation*
Historically, most successful national or regional movements have had one thing in common — they were well-organised at the grass roots level. It is this local participation and organisation that provides the greatest chance for success throughout the South as a whole. The Fortress Dixie Southern Website Directory provides a list of several Southern national organisation chapters in your city or state.

54 *If No Local Chapter or Camp Exists in Your Area, Then Start One Today!*
If you live in a location where there is not a local SCV camp or LOS county or city organisation, consider contacting the state leadership of the SCV or LOS in order to get a local presence started. Read Michael Hill's *How To Start A Local LOS County Organisation* or contact the state headquarters of the organisations in which you are interested. For example, where I live, the North Carolina Southern Party and the North Carolina League of the South are actively promoting cross-membership and chapters in both organisations throughout the state.

Suggestions for Southern Heritage Defense

55 Refer to Southern Heritage Groups as "Civil Rights Organisations"

The anti-Southern forces have stolen the debate by virtue of stealing the language. Southerners have civil rights, too, and our heritage groups fight to protect them just as the NAACP purports to do for people of colour. Other civil rights groups (such as the NAACP and the Southern Poverty Law Centre) do not hold a patent on the term "civil rights."

You may also consider giving them a taste of their own medicine by referring to Dixie's antagonists as "radical" groups on the "fringe of society."

56 Fight All Heritage Violations

Although individual, local action is always important to defend against attacks on our heritage, I urge all concerned Southerners to multiply their efforts by working through appropriate organisations. Consider supporting the following:

- **Southern Legal Resource Centre**
  The SLRC, headed by Kirk Lyons, is the most important and feared Southern civil rights organisation in the United States. He is a personal friend and I urge every reader to get on the SLRC e-mail list and send a contribution to help fund the organisation's overwhelming heritage defence activities. I would also urge you to sign up for a monthly pledge to the SLRC. While I do not agree with Kirk on every issue, he is fearless, honourable (sometimes to a fault), and a real Southern leader whom we all can support. In addition, Kirk can get along with anyone

and his mediation has been helpful in many fights and disagreements among compatriots in the Southern Movement.

- **Southern Caucus**
 This political website is dedicated to helping individual Southerners defend the proud history of the Confederacy and celebrate our forefathers' sacrifices and beliefs in state sovereignty and limited, constitutional government.

- **Heritage Preservation Association**
 The HPA is a national nonprofit membership organisation utilising educational resources in conjunction with legal and political action to protect and preserve the symbols, culture, and heritage of the American South. The HPA has members in forty-nine states and six countries and chapters in ten states.

- **Southern Anti-Bigotry Coalition**
 This is a Internet-based effort to counter bigotry against Southern heritage in the media.

- **Southern Heritage of the Carolinas**
 This group (organised and led by Vickie Poston) has won many victories for the South and has helped preserve Southern heritage in North and South Carolina. Please consider lending them your support.

Suggestions for Southern Heritage Defense

57 *Contact Your Southern Organisation's Heritage Defence Officer*
Offer your time, personal efforts, and funding to those who carry the struggle day and night to defend the proud heritage of Dixie. Get involved in this sacred crusade to defend Southern heritage and symbols while fighting for the same constitutional republic for which our Confederate ancestors gave their all. Contact your local and state organisations and get involved now before it is too late. If you are a member of the SCV, for example, contact:

    Roger McCredie,
    Chief of Heritage Defence
    P.O. Box 18152
    Asheville, NC 28814
    Tel: (828) 254-6991 Fax: 828-254-4534
    E-mail: rebscape@bellsouth.net

58 *Organise an Annual Confederate Holiday Event in Your Local Community*
Celebrate Confederate Memorial Day or organise a Jefferson Davis, Robert E. Lee, or Stonewall Jackson parade or supper. Do not limit yourself to the historical holidays; follow the example of those down in Columbia, South Carolina, where there will now be an annual heritage event celebrating the successful Columbia Flag Rally.

You may also want to consider throwing parties or backyard barbecues to celebrate Southern holidays such as the anniversary of the battle at Fort Sumter, the Battle of Chancellorsville, or the day your home state seceded. Most people need little excuse to attend a party and you can use the opportunity to educate and instil some

Southern Pride in your friends and neighbours. It is also a grand opportunity to indulge in some good ol' Southern cookin'! (By the way, it is not a bad idea to buy a Southern cookbook, either.)

59 *Request the Permission of Local Merchants to Install Pro-South Displays*

Check with your local stores, service stations, and merchants to see if they will allow you to place Confederate brochures or petitions in their places of business. Be respectful and thank them even if they refuse.

60 *Ask Others to Fly Our Flag!*

Contact your local mobile home park and automobile dealerships that tend to fly only the flag of the Washington government and ask that they also fly their state flag. You may also ask them to fly a Confederate flag but this may prove to be an insurmountable obstacle. (If they are unwilling to fly the Battle flag or Third National flag, ask them to consider the Stars and Bars instead.) If you want to be more creative still, pose as a customer and indicate your dissatisfaction at purchasing a product at a business that flies only the federal flag.

61 *Adopt a Confederate Monument or Cemetery*

Then clean it up, keep it up, and help protect it from vandals. If you cannot find a local Confederate cemetery, consider supporting the Oakwood Cemetery, which is the final resting place of more than seventeen thousand Confederate heroes in Richmond, Virginia. For more information or to make a donation, write to:

Suggestions for Southern Heritage Defense

Oakwood Confederate Cemetery Trust, Inc.
P.O. Box 8494
Richmond, VA 23226.

Remember the words of Robert E. Lee: "The graves of the Confederate dead will always be green in my memory, and their deeds hallowed in my recollection."

<u>62</u> *Create Our Own "Southern" Sports Team*
Local SCV, LOS, and state Southern Party organisations should attempt to field or financially support little league and other sports teams with the local camp or organisation emblem and website address prominently displayed on the uniforms. In doing so we contribute to the community and go on the offensive against the PC crowd.

<u>63</u> *Raise Money to Build a New Confederate Monument in Your Community*
While few of us can match Jack Kershaw's magnificent Nathan Bedford Forrest Statue and Flag Park in Nashville, Tennessee, we can band together with friends and other Confederate organisations to build new monuments throughout Dixie. Try to keep in step with tradition by having any statues stand with their backs to the North. Always keep in mind that there is *nothing* the other side hates more than new Southern monuments!

<u>64</u> *Wear a Third National Flag Lapel Pin*
While I always wear a small flag at Southern events, I often leave it on for business meetings and sometimes at church. As of now, I have never received a negative comment (I am sure standing six-foot-three probably helps). It really does start a number of interesting con-

versations about Dixie because most people are not really sure what the Third National flag is. Try wearing a small lapel pin and see what happens.

65 Start a Southern Shooting Club
Exercise your Second Amendment rights (our Confederate forefathers certainly did). Learn proper gun safety and proficiency and meet more pro-gun, pro-Confederate friends and neighbours.

66 Set Up a Southern Booth or Table at Local Events
Set up an information table or booth and hand out flyers at local fairs, gun shows, flea markets, and other events attended by conservatives and pro-heritage people. Contact Jack Clark, Chairman of the Southern Party of North Carolina at jack@spnc.org to learn about their success with local booths and information tables.

67 Do You Know a Good Lawyer?
While our adversaries have often used the corrupted American legal system against Southern interests, some honourable pro-South lawyers are flocking to the Cause to defend Southern heritage and symbols. If you know a skilled and honourable lawyer with Southern sympathies, introduce them to the newly formed Southern Bar Association:

    Mr. Jack Kershaw
    (615) 292-2316
    Don Bustion
    Executive Director
    SBA
    P.O. Box 954

Magnolia, AR 71754
Kershaw@magnolia-net.com

Kirk Lyons
Southern Legal Resource Centre
P.O. Box 1235
Black Mountain, NC 28711
(828) 669-5189
slrc@cheta.net.

68 *Start a Southern Heritage Business*
Why not promote Southern heritage through the sale of flags, bumper stickers, books, and so forth, and make some money at the same time? Check with your tax advisor, but you should be able to deduct your trips to Southern conferences and reenactments where you set up a table and promote your business.

69 *If They Fly One Flag, We Will Fly Two*
Whenever you see a home or business flying the Stars and Stripes, stop and give them a small flag of your state and region and respectfully ask that they also remember these as well. Always remember to be pleasant and respectful of their opinions. After all, it is their right to fly whatever flag they choose on private property.

70 *Work Together for Dixie*
Work with other pro-South groups in your area, encouraging cross-memberships with other organisations. To find other pro-South organisations in your area, refer to the Fortress Dixie Southern Website Directory.

Chapter Five

Action Ideas for Southern Activists

When organising a protest or rally, it is important to always be polite, respectful of authority, and equipped with the required permits and permission. Above all, control who marches and pickets, how they dress, and the content of their signs and banners. Your failure to monitor and control a heritage event, protest, march, or celebration could make the event a public relations disaster. Also, make sure you have a designated public spokesman to handle any media interviews.

The media are, in general, against our message. They will interview the worst possible spokesman and record and photograph the worst-dressed participants. If you do not control your message and your event, the media will.

71 *March and Rally for Dixie*
Attend and participate in Southern heritage marches and rallies similar to the ones held recently in Columbia, South Carolina, and Montgomery, Alabama. Strive to be on hand at other rallies scheduled for other locations in the future. We must seize the initiative.

72 *Picket for Dixie*
Thousands of proud Southerners all across Dixie have picketed and marched in defence of Southern symbols and Southern rights. One recent and well-known victory was led by Vickie Poston, head of Southern Heritage of the Carolinas, and took place in Badin, North Carolina. Vickie and many volunteers launched a months-long protest against Alcoa for that company's discrimination against its Southern employees. You might be surprised at what can be accomplished when just a few brave Southerners "take to the streets" — even against a large, multinational corporation such as Alcoa.

73 *Become a One-Person Protest For Dixie*
If you have the courage, do an H. K. Edgerton-style protest. On many a long, cold winter day, he has stood at Pack Square in front of my office proudly wearing a Confederate uniform while brandishing a Third National flag in one hand and a sign reading "Heritage, Not Hate" in the other. He is a true Southern patriot — a person whom I am proud to call my friend and compatriot. Read the first (and last) poem I have ever written,

"Tribute to H. K. Edgerton," at my website, www.ronholland.com/hk.htm.

74 *Be Prepared for a Reaction*

Make it a habit to carry an inexpensive disposable camera or, better still, to have audio- and video-recording equipment with you. Always ask to see the identification of the press or police authorities that may be present and be sure to note their names and affiliation. They will treat your much more kindly if they know that you know who they are. To be polite always ask them for whom they work and in what city they live. Again, be certain to have all necessary permits and permission you may need to mount a rally or protest.

Twenty years (and thirty pounds) ago I was involved in a protest at the U.S. Snail (post office) without permit and permission. Approximately five minutes into the protest, police cars arrived on each corner of the street where we were protesting (we were on public property). The cops jumped out and gave us the choice of leaving immediately or going to jail. (Just guess which option we chose.) Do not let this happen to you.

75 *Give a Speech, but Write It Down*

During the summer of 2000 award-winning columnist Charlie Reese and I spoke at an LOS meeting down in Brunswick, Georgia. Some governmental bureaucratic-types accused us of saying something "improper" about secession and the U.S. government. What they did not know was that my speech was written down and on the Internet, so I dared them to show where I had stated anything wrong. We heard nothing more from them! Although speaking off the cuff is fun (unless the speech is to be taped), always speak from a written draft so that no one is able to put words in your mouth or twist what you say to advance the agenda of the Political Establishment.

76 *Fight Racism and the Misuse of Our Sacred Southern Symbols at Every Opportunity*
Some people speak against Southern heritage because our flags have sometimes been misappropriated by insidious hate groups such as the Ku Klux Klan and neo-Nazis. They do have a point. White supremacist groups have abused our symbols in the past, causing modern-day Southerners to pay the price for this by suffering attacks on our heritage. We must act quickly and oppose any fringe group, such as the Klan, that misappropriates our symbols.

77 *Keep a Journal of Your Confederate Activities*
The struggle for Dixie will probably go on for many years as we defend our heritage and Confederate Nation from attacks by the most powerful force on the face of the earth today. Our children and grandchildren may well be motivated to continue the struggle by reading our Southern journals many years in the future. In an evil, dark future, when all honest history, monuments, and memorials about Dixie are buried, our private journals may be the spark to ignite another activist generation in defence of Southern Rights. Our battle for Dixie today is just as important as our ancestors' defence of the Confederacy over 140 years ago. Help ensure that future generations of Southerners know about our struggle for Southern freedom and the Constitution.

Action Ideas for Southern Activists

<u>78</u> *Tip Well and Leave More than Money*
Consider leaving a Confederate flyer of your choice at every meal when you dine out. I once read in an Ann Landers column where a well-meaning Christian was leaving Christian tracts in lieu of tips at restaurants. This is a sure way to turn off someone who makes their living off of tips. Leave an appropriate brochure and tip well if you want the waiter to read the material.

<u>79</u> *When Travelling, Make Every Rest Stop a Sales Opportunity for Dixie*
Every rest area and bathroom stall is an appropriate place to leave brochures; hand out material to others you meet at the location or service station and distribute self-adhesive messages about the Cause. Of course, always remember to respect private and public property. Vandalism wins few converts and dishonours our message.

Chapter Six

Southern Economic & Financial Actions

Put Your Money in Dixie ~ Where Your Heart Is!

We know that we cannot depend on others to look out for Dixie, so we need to do it ourselves. The quickest way to grab the attention of people and corporate interests is through their wallets. We should invest in Southern concerns and shy away from giving our time and money to businesses outside of Dixie or those unreceptive to our Cause.

80 *Support "Real Southern Businesses" and Businessmen*
Support Southern merchants like Maurice Bessinger and buy from other pro-South businesses listed in the Fortress Dixie Southern Heritage Products and Services Website.

You may want to consider asking for Southern products when frequenting restaurants. (Do you have any Texas wines on the menu?) In addition, be sure to check labels when shopping for groceries; buy Dixie when you can.

81 *Start a Local "Buy Southern" Program*
Start a local campaign that encourages others to buy Southern, local products and services. Your local farmers and merchants will love this. Discourage people from doing business with out-of-state chain stores that drive locals out of business and hurt the "Little Man." Some of these chains include Wal-Mart (an Arkansas company that has since sold Dixie down the river), McDonalds, Burger King, and . . . well, you know who they are. Not only will you help the local economy, but eating fresh, local produce and avoiding "Yankee fast foods" will help you to live healthier and longer in order to defend Dixie. This is the ultimate revenge.

82 *Support Local Charities Only*
Support only local charities so that you can determine how and where your donations are used. Shy away from charities that tend to promote social agendas rather than helping those who are truly in need.

83 *Privately Help Needy Confederates*
Provide assistance (financial or otherwise) for new parents who are local Southerners. We need to populate the South with Confederates, but having large families is often a strain on the resources of young couples. Likewise, follow what the Lord commands us in the Book of James by helping (Southern) orphans and widows.

Southern Economic & Financial Actions

Also, be sure not to neglect your fellow Confederate activists; oftentimes they lose their jobs because of their support for the Cause. Help them out if you can.

84 *Be On the Lookout for New and Better Jobs for Confederate Friends*
We all could use a promotion! Or perhaps we just need to upgrade our working skills through additional on-the-job training, technical school, or university education. If you learn of a job opening and know a local Confederate that would better fill the position, pass the job lead down to him or her. The better our employment, the more money we make, the more extra time we have, the better we can support the Cause. It is as simple as that.

85 *Be Aware of Anti-South Conspiracy in Commercial Enterprise*
Never forget that the South Carolina Chamber of Commerce strongly supported taking the Confederate flag down in South Carolina. Don't forget the corporate conspiracy of national retailers like Wal-mart to put Maurice Bessinger out of business. Make them pay by taking your business elsewhere. See number 92.

86 *Buy Stock in Anti-South Corporations*
If you own stock in Wal-Mart or other anti-South corporate giants, you have every right to attend and voice your opinions at the annual stockholders meeting. Large public corporations hate bad publicity and disruptive stockholders most of all. (Besides, you could end up holding enough stock one day to direct corporate policy!)

__87__ *Receive a Tax Deduction by Supporting Freedom in Dixie*
You can receive a tax deduction for your financial contribution to a number of tax-exempt 501(c) 3 organisations to defend Dixie, the Constitution, freedom, and the free market. We can all use tax deductions; I consider that every "red cent" that I am forced to give to Uncle Sam will be used against liberty, the South, and constitutional government. The SLRC, Mary K. Noel Foundation, Rockford Institute, Ludwig von Mises Institute, and SCV are examples of such organisations.

Please note that many Dixie-friendly organisations have political restraints placed upon them by Washington in return for the tax deductibility of your contributions. They have strict tax guidelines to follow and their reluctance to become too politically engaged often stems more from a regulatory requirement than anything else.

__88__ *Contribute Extra Funds to Your Favourite Southern Organisations*
The LOS, SCV, and other organisations can use your contributions over and above their standard membership dues. Remember, when it comes to lobbying the public, money accounts for almost everything.

__89__ *Advertise in Pro-South Publications, Websites, and at Southern Events*
Each of us can advertise our businesses on pro-Southern websites and publications, as well as on display tables at Southern events. This usually will enable you to deduct your advertising as a business expense. Remember, most meetings have a conference brochure that sells advertising space.

Southern Economic & Financial Actions

90 *Deal With Local Banks and Southern Financial Institutions*

Try to deal with hometown financial institutions rather than distant, multinational organisations. I am sure you understand that an institution being headquartered nominally in Dixie, like Wal-mart or Bank of America (the old NationsBank, formerly North Carolina National Bank), means nothing here. As a Southern investment consultant and financial writer, I can assist you if you have questions about what businesses are "real" Southern businesses. Feel free to e-mail me at:

Ronholland@compuserve.com.

91 *Control Your Personal Debt and Pay off Your Bills*

Massive personal debt puts your debtors in charge of your financial future rather than yourself. Resist the easy credit offered today by financial institutions because too much personal debt can destroy your freedom of choice and personal liberty just as surely as an out-of-control federal government can. My advice is to pay off your consumer debt, and even your home mortgage, before investing heavily in the stock market or other investments. Interest adds up day and night, day upon day. As Albert Einstein noted, compound interest is one of the wonders of the world. That is true if you are earning interest, but it works the other way, too, if you have too much debt.

92 *Boycott Anti-South Businesses*

While I believe in free markets and freedom of action, it will be a long time before I do business with corporate giants like Wal-Mart and the supermarket chains that boycotted Maurice Bessinger's products. Some legal experts indicate these corporations "may have" engaged in a conspiracy to put Maurice Bessinger out of business because he dared stand up to the powerful political elite and chamber of commerce special interests that wanted the Confederate flag on the South Carolina capitol dome removed. While the New York and international owners of these businesses have the right to sell or not to sell any product, for any reason, this well-timed and co-ordinated action concerns me because of its monopolistic appearance of impropriety. It is rumoured that the case will eventually come before the courts and that, just maybe, Mr. Bessinger will receive fair and honourable treatment from the legal system. But you should not hold your breath.

93 *Protect Your Family and Property Against Lawsuit*
Due to America's corrupted, broken legal system we have become the lawsuit capital of the world. Every person with savings, a home, or property are at risk from slanderous lawsuits, unfair court judgments, and unconstitutional government asset seizures. I suggest that you educate yourself about the risks and different ways in which you can legally protect your assets by linking to the Asset Protection and Financial Privacy Website Directory.

Beware of any Confederates that might sue or threaten to use litigation against another Confederate. Using the corrupted U.S. legal system to adjudicate disagreements between Confederates that should be settled by arbitration or disinterested third parties is bad news for

Southern Economic & Financial Actions

the Southern Movement. If you are suspicious of lawyers and the direction the U.S. legal system has taken, then refer to our anti-lawyer quotes on Ron Holland's Politically Incorrect Freedom Quotes.

94 *Pay Your Bills with Confederate Cheques*

Consider ordering Confederate cheques from Olde South Limited in South Carolina. You will be making a statement every time you pay your bills with five attractive varieties of Confederate design cheques.

95 *Pay Bills with Confederate Credit Cards*

Current SCV members can obtain such a credit card and we are now working with several other organisations to be able to offer Confederate credit card services to Southerners who want to promote Confederate symbols whenever they pay by credit card. Remember only to use a credit card if you are planning to pay off the entire balance at the end of the month. Stay out of debt!

96 *Just as You Tithe to the Lord, Give to Dixie*

The people and organisations defending Dixie can only win the battle if we contribute enough money to the Cause. I urge you to ponder and pray about how much you should contribute to the Movement — then do so on a regular monthly or quarterly basis. The more regular the income of organisations like the SCV, LOS, SLRC, and others, the better each can budget for the future defence of Southern heritage, rights, and self-determination for Dixie.

Chapter Seven

Political & Lobbying Activities

Some of our greatest victories can be achieved not by fighting against the system but by working within it. A primary reason that our traditional civil and political institutions have gone astray is because too many of us have neglected our rights and our duties as citizens for too long.

We can advance the Southern Cause in leaps and bounds merely by exercising the rights and privileges that our ancestors fought and died to gain or preserve.

97 *Register to Vote*

The ballot box is our greatest weapon in forwarding our Cause, and we should use it. If you are not currently registered to vote, you should register immediately. You may register wherever you obtain a driver's license, at many U.S. Post Offices, and, in some states, you can register to vote via the Internet. It's fast, easy, and convenient. After you have registered, make sure that your Confederate friends and neighbours are registered. Above all, make sure you vote — make your voice heard. Make our leaders accountable for their actions.

98 *E-mail the Members of Your State Legislature on Important Confederate Issues*
Virtually every politician and government entity has an e-mail account these days. It is arguably the easiest, most convenient vehicle for voicing your opinions and concerns to your elected officials. You should flood their offices with e-mails in favour of Southern issues. But remember that officeholders are still leaders, and, therefore, they deserve to be treated with respect. Always send tactful and intelligent messages.

99 *Learn More about Political Action*
Educate yourself about political action and strategy. There are numerous foundations and websites that provide valuable information in this area. (Refer to Appendix A.)

100 *Consider Political Action for Dixie*
Choose your party, whether it is the Reform, Libertarian, Constitution, Southern, or other pro-South and pro-freedom political action groups. If you do not want to go the third party route, consider recruiting someone

Political & Lobbying Activities

to run as a pro-independence heritage candidate in the Democrat or Republican parties.

101 *Run for Office Yourself*
Consider running for political office personally to advance the cause of Dixie. While there is little chance of getting elected on a pro-independence/ heritage platform this early in the game, your campaign can help to spread ideas of preserving Southern heritage and securing self-determination for Dixie. Running for a seat on the local school board or for sheriff are often the best ways to have an impact on rural Southern life.

102 *E-mail Congress and the Washington Politicians (Including the President)*
Now with free internet technology you can let our "leaders" in Washington know exactly what you think about issues and how they represent you. Please be sure to communicate with them often on the issues that concern Dixie (but, again, be respectful).

103 *Lobby the Politicians in Washington, Your State, and at the Local Level*
WorldNetDaily.com provides an excellent resource base through which you can contact federal and state legislators by phone, fax, snail mail, and e-mail on pertinent issues. Keep your lawmakers abreast of current attacks on Dixie through frequent e-mails and forwarded copies of Internet and newspaper articles or editorials.

104 *Inform Local Politicians That Less Federal Power Means More Local Power*
As LOS president Dr. Michael Hill writes, "this appeal works with most politicians (when they have taken the time to reflect on it)." Suggest that they read Dr. Thomas Naylor's *Downsizing the USA*. Remind them that they are politicians and that more local power and programs means more for them to do.

This raises an important question: If all politicians are the same, what is the benefit of local and regional governments? The benefit is that a local politician generally shares more of your local concerns, needs, and objectives than a distant politician out of Washington, D.C. Second, since a local politician lives relatively nearby they tend to be more responsive and understanding of your needs and wishes. If you do not agree with your local politician, just go visit him or her. It is far easier to demand accountability from a politician that you can "get your hands on."

105 *Make Every Anti-South Politician's Day a Bad One*
Remember that the politicians belonging to the federal, state, and local political establishments continue to steal our wealth and freedoms each and every day. At the same time, they simultaneously represent the special interest groups at the expense of productive, working Americans. Try to find a few minutes each day to send an e-mail to several of the most "wretched" politicians that claim to represent your interests so they will know that we will never forget their callous disregard for us or our historic constitutional freedoms.

Political & Lobbying Activities

106 *Be Prepared for Anti-South Propaganda*
Historical accuracy, truth, and justice often mean nothing to the Anti-South portions of the Political Establishment. Do not expect fair treatment — this is a total cultural war against Dixie. When they twist our words, insult us and our families, make fun of our religious faith, call us names, and attempt to label us with vile and offensive names, understand that their goal is to frustrate and humiliate Southerners into giving up. These lies are simply propaganda designed to destroy our ideals, symbols, and beliefs.

Remember that in the United States today, propaganda is not distributed by the government but by its willing accomplices NBC, CBS, ABC, CNN, and your local newspaper and television affiliates. Most of the media are simply the propaganda surrogates used by the political elite against everything Southern.

107 *Know and Publicise Your Washington Politician's Voting Record*
Get a congressional report card on your representatives in Congress. The Congressional Report Cards website provides this information. You can now get data on all the Congressional votes since 1991 by visiting the Voter Information Service database.

108 *Offer to Work in Local Political Campaigns for Conservative, Pro-South Candidates*
Although computers and the Internet can help our communications, knowledge, and education, without plain, old-fashioned political action, nothing will get done. Internet-based actions alone will never protect your

liberty or get our constitutional republic back. Get involved in politics, make contacts, and let the conservative politicians who share our values learn that Southern nationalists and heritage defenders can contribute much to their campaigns and the entire political process. Besides what better way is there to gain access to a politician than by joining their staff (even if it is just as a volunteer)?

109 Make Financial Contributions to Pro-South Political Candidates

Running for public office is an exensive proposition. Be quick to lend a hand financially when a pro-South candidate throws his or her hat in the ring.

110 Get Involved with the Two Major Political Parties to Promote Our Cause

While I certainly am not a fan of the corrupt two-party monopoly that controls the entire political process in the United States, there is a limit to how effectively most third party efforts can contribute to our Cause at present. I certainly would prefer to live in a union ruled under the auspices of the Constitution, Southern, or even the Libertarian parties, but that is not to be — for now.

We must face the fact that most third parties receive little more than two percent of the vote in most elections. Contributing large sums of money to such efforts is often a waste of limited campaign contributions and efforts. While it is important (and necessary) to build third party movements in preparation for the day when they will make a real impact for Southern political action, the promotional and educational benefits of publicising our Cause in Republican primary elections far outweigh most third party election efforts. All political activity for Dixie can help, but you have to decide what course of action and which political party effort is best for you. I believe that the Republican party stands as our best choice (for now) for achieving meaningful political goals for the defence of Dixie.

111 *Help One of the New Southern Political Parties Get on the Ballot*

Offer your services to the new Southern political parties advocating self-determination for Dixie. Petitioning for ballot access is the only way new political parties can get on the ballot in most states. Remember, a third political party is nothing more than a discussion group until it gets on the ballot and fields candidates. Contact the chapter of one of the Southern political parties in your state and get involved today. The Fortress Dixie Southern Political Parties List provides valuable contact information. New Southern political parties are always forming. If you know of a new effort that is not listed, please send the new effort's URL to Fortress Dixie.

Although I encourage you to support the new individual state Southern Party organisations, I do not suggest that you support or condone the divisive actions of a few remaining leaders of the national Southern Party organisation. If you would like more information or insight into the circumstances surrounding the Southern Party fissure, please review Jim Langcuster's "Views on the Southern Party Debacle," available at www.home-rule-for-dixie.com/reading/debacle.html (Jim was the author of the "Asheville Declaration") and "My Southern Party Story" by Patrick Leslie (one of the original signers of the Asheville Declaration), available at www.maitreg.com/South/SP/Leslie/index.asp.

112 *Get Involved in Local Conservative Causes and Organisations*
If you want to meet fellow Confederates and others who share your conservative Christian views, refer to the list of websites in the appendix. Volunteer to assist with the campaign of a conservative candidate. Nearly all conservatives are good candidates for the Southern movement.

113 *Prepare Local Scoreboards on the Voting of Your Local Politicians*
While most citizens neither know nor care to know how their "so-called" representatives vote on issues, many conservative Southerners that could be attracted to our Cause are interested. Local SCV camps, LOS chapters, and other state and county organisations could assist in such an endeavour to promote their organisations while simultaneously educating the voters on how to vote Southern in the future. Visit the Voter Information Services to know how well your elected representatives are (or are not) representing your Southern interests.

114 *Pass along the Tips in this Manual to Your Southern Friends and Compatriots*
I strongly encourage you to pass along the advice in this manual to your friends and brothers-in-arms. We must work together to promote and defend Dixie and our Southern way of life. Plant a seed and watch it grow!

Political & Lobbying Activities

This work is only a small part of a larger, more in-depth book I have written entitled *Confederate Nation* that will be available soon on the Internet and as an affordable paperback, again for maximum distribution.

115 *Attend Local Government Meetings*

"The squeaky wheel gets the grease" is an old saying, but it is still as true as the first time it was uttered. Nothing frightens elected officials more than active, informed voters who hold them accountable. Make it a habit to attend city and county council meetings, as well as those of your local school board. Make your voice heard and promote the Southern view.

116 *Start a Petition Drive in Your Local Community*

How many times have you walked into a service station or local store and seen a petition drive on a local or Southern heritage issue? Consider starting one in your area. Not only is this a great way to promote your organisation or a heritage issue, it can also be used to build a mailing list of local citizens that favour Confederate and conservative causes. Be sure to add a place on the petition for an address, telephone number, and e-mail address.

Chapter Eight

Media and Press Actions

Although the mainstream media are generally not receptive to the Southern message, they do respond to the bottom line. The media outlets depend upon advertising revenue to remain in business. In turn, the revenue depends upon ratings — how many readers, viewers, or listeners each program has.

By alerting the newspapers and networks to your displeasure at their reporting on Southern issues, or better still, by indicating that you and others will no longer subscribe to their paper or watch/ listen to their programme, you can rest assured that you will (eventually) gain their attention.

117 *E-mail the Media*
Make your views known to newspapers, radio, and television media. Use World Net Daily's "Guide to the Media" to contact major print and broadcast news outlets with news releases and editorials concerning attacks on Southern heritage. Remember that polite, carefully reasoned, and well-written material will increase your likelihood of success. The best media guide is online through Congress.org, where you can e-mail specific print and broadcast media in any of the United States. Two other options are the Conservative Caucus Press List and World Net Daily's Newspaper List. I also urge you to create a news release list of all the print, radio, and television media in your state — and use it often.

118 *Listen to and Call in to Talk Radio and Television Programmes*
If you have the time, monitor talk radio or watch call-in programs on CNN, CNBC, Fox News Channel, and C-Span. Try to phone in or e-mail occasional questions and responses concerning Southern heritage issues.

119 *Write to the Newspaper*
Write letters to the editor and guest editorials anytime you see an anti-Southern or anti-flag article or column. Send the newspaper editor a reasoned, polite correspondence by e-mail or regular mail expressing your dissent. Post the offending message to others so they can join in a letter-writing, faxing, telephoning, and e-mailing campaign. Do your best to obtain the offending writer's regular mail address and telephone number, as telephone calls and mail to one's place of business are far

more effective than e-mail. Remember to be polite and offer carefully reasoned rebuttals to their opinions. Be mindful that they are as much entitled to their opinions as you are. Moreover, avoid personal attacks. Keep it short; as Shakespeare wrote: "Brevity is the soul of wit."

120 *Thank Columnists for Fair and Balanced Articles*
This is important. Most columnists write negative articles on Dixie to curry favour with their editors or the owners of their publications. It takes courage and conviction to risk one's job and advancement by going against the PC crowd. These brave members of the press deserve our support and gratitude.

121 *Agree to an Interview with the Press*
Do not accept every interview with the press. The old saying that "all press coverage, good or bad, is beneficial" is wrong. Before agreeing to an in-depth interview, check the press member's credentials, ask for previous articles they have written on Southern heritage events, and so forth. If you feel comfortable, proceed with the interview; if you do not, politely decline. If you decline, suggest someone you feel may be more appropriate. Too many people have lost their jobs (or worse) due to bad, vicious, or untrue reporting.

Be prepared for the "ringer question." The initial questions are usually fair and objective but the latter may be inappropriatly designed to make you or Dixie look bad. If the question is biased or unfair, simply answer the question with a question aimed back at the interviewer. Finally, always repeat the question during your response to give you time to think about the right answer and to rephrase any unfair or misleading questions.

<u>122</u> *Create and Monitor a List of Anti-South Press Contacts*
While all of the major Establishment press organisations and reporters are virulently anti-Confederate, pro-big government, and liberal, some will still do their best to write a fair and balanced interview. Their best may not be enough to satisfy us, but sometimes an interview or article that shows both sides of a story will get our message across in spite of the obstacles.

Many members of the press will deliberately set out to soil the South and our heritage by asking leading questions and launching dishonest, personal attacks in attempts to label good, honest, and patriotic Southerners as racists, closet Klansmen, and so forth. This is a favourite tactic of the left-leaning political and media Establishment. Therefore, we need a list of dishonest people in the press who do not give Southern heritage a fair hearing or balanced reporting so that we will know what to expect when they approach us. All press interviews with these reprobates should be declined; there are plenty of fair reporters who will attempt to report all sides of an issue and give the people of Dixie a fair shake. This is the most we can ask from the media Establishment.

Please e-mail the Southern Caucus at Ronholland@compuserve.com when you observe prejudiced, anti-Dixie articles in the press so that we may monitor and publish a list of anti-Southern journalists and publications on the Internet.

Media and Press Actions

123 *Boycott the Biased Media Establishment*
Do not give the media Establishment your hard-earned money in return for their biased reporting and editorials. Boycott big liberal newspapers and those of your local newspapers that you know to be owned by distant, liberal media conglomerates. For fair and honest reporting, refer to the Unbiased Conservative Internet News Sites for Southerners list on the Fortress Dixie website.

Chapter Nine

Utilise the Internet

The marvel of modern technology puts a new world at our fingertips. On the Information Superhighway, we in the Southern Movement can gather information in unprecedented amounts and from a myriad of sources. The days of having "news" spoon-fed to us by our local newspaper and the three major television networks are gone.

In addition, the Internet enables us to communicate with media contacts, political representatives, and one another like never before. Most important, however, is the power of the Internet to help us mobilise in such numbers and with such speed so as to keep our opponents off-balance and continually guessing at what we will be doing next!

124 *Arm Yourself with a Personal Computer*

Our opponents have near total control over the media Establishment which prevents a fair and open discussion of our viewpoint in the battle to defend Southern heritage. The Establishment will almost always report an event unfairly and attempt to show the defenders of Dixie in the worst possible light and situation.

The best way to get out the truth about Dixie is to own a personal computer and visit honest, conservative news sites that will present the story in a fair and unbiased manner. The media monopoly and blackout means you cannot read our side of the story unless you have a computer. Remember that all national news outlets, including most local newspapers, radio, and television stations, are owned and controlled by large media conglomerates that dictate how news is to be presented. Do not let the Establishment media spoon-feed you their liberal propaganda. Seek the real news for yourself. The Truth is out there.

125 *Add a Confederate Screen Saver to Your Home or Office Computer*

South-art.com has developed a number of fantastic Confederate-oriented screen savers; visit their website for free downloads of several attractive graphics. There are a plethora of sources for Southern clip art on the Internet if you just take the time to seek them out.

Utilise the Internet

126 *Vote in Internet Polls*
Participate in every Southern cultural and flag "referendum" on the Internet. These polls are mentioned frequently on the Aw Shucks website and on many Southern e-mail lists. Some will only allow you to vote once while others have no limitations. As some crooked politicians in the two main parties used to say, "Vote early and vote often."

127 *Sign Up for Southern E-mail News Lists*
Stay current with Southern heritage news and events around Dixie by signing joining an e-mail list. Many of the Southern heritage websites, such as LewRockwell.com and those belonging to LOS and SCV have e-mail list serves to which you may subscribe.

128 *Create Your Own Southern E-mail List*
Do you have a number of Southern compatriots with whom you correspond frequently via e-mail? If so, you might consider creating your own e-mail list to help Southerners in your local area or region stay abreast of heritage attacks or events. Of course you should also use your site to co-ordinate the defence of Southern symbols and monuments.

129 *Build a Personal Southern Website*
It has never been easier to build your own website than it is right now. Internet publishing programs such as Front Page make it easier than ever to get your own site up and running. Once your site is ready, contact Fortress Dixie so we can list you in the appropriate category, thereby increasing the traffic to your site. The Fortress Dixie

Southern Website Directory currently lists more than two thousand Southern sites on the Internet — yours should be one of them.

Frankly, I knew little about websites or surfing the Web when I began doing both in late 1999. Since then I have built several pro-South websites to help defend Dixie.

If you feel that you need the help of a professional web page designer, you may want to consider contacting Jeff McCormick, the webmaster for Dixienet.org. Jeff can provide the assistance you need to create an attractive (and informative) Southern site. He can be reached at:
apologia@dixienet.org.

130 *Fight Racism and the Misuse of Our Sacred Southern Symbols on Your Website*
Our opponents try to falsely paint the Southern Movement's supporters and our Confederate symbols as racist. Although it is clear to us that indiscriminately labelling proud Southerners as racists is dishonest and intellectually lazy, it is not always clear to others. During the height of the Cold War a political adversary could be easily discredited by accusing him or her of being a Communist (whether it was true or not). Those who speak out against Dixie attempt to soil us and our Cause by painting us with the broad brush of racism. We cannot — we must not — allow them to employ this red herring to distract from our message and our Cause.

There is no room for hatred or racism in the Southern Movement. If you harbour either in your heart, you are not welcome here. Therefore, conduct yourself appropriately. We in the Southern Movement are (unfairly)

Utilise the Internet

judged by a narrow standard. Do not provide the other side with any ammunition. Consider adding an anti-hate graphic on your website. Again, South-art.com has created the best anti-racist graphic on the Internet. Go to their site to get the graphic; be sure to give credit to South Art and link to their site.

Make it clear to all like-minded Southerners, of all races, that they are welcome within our ranks. The South is a place, not a race. Remember, we are all brothers and sisters of Dixie.

131 *Join Southern Internet Discussion and List Serve Groups*

Participate in Southern-oriented discussion groups where you can meet and get to know other Southerners who believe in defending Dixie and our heritage. More importantly, get involved with other conservative, libertarian, and free market discussion groups where you can actually promote our Cause and gain new converts in the battle to defend Dixie.

Remember it is easy to be aggressive and negative in e-mail correspondence. Even fellow Confederates who are usually mild-mannered and considerate can make this mistake. I, too, have been guilty of this transgression. Practise the First Southern Internet Commandment that demands that we always behave like Southern ladies and gentlemen. Passion for the Cause is one thing, rude and abrasive behaviour is quite another.

132 *Add Your Website to Existing Southern Web Rings for More Traffic*

Go to the Yahoo! Web ring and search under "Dixie," "Confederate," "Southern," and so forth. There are more

than thirty Web rings (of which I am aware) that are oriented toward the Southern Movement and/or the War for Southern Independence. Yahoo Webring:
http://dir.webring.yahoo.com/rw

133 *Create Your Own Southern Web Ring*
The best manner in which to be certain that a good Southern Web ring exists is to create your own and become a Confederate ringmaster! You will then attract more traffic to your own site, connect your site with others of similar interest, and help to develop an online community of Southern sites.

134 *Start an Online Petition on Southern Issues*
Go to www.petitiononline.com, which provides free online hosting of public petitions for responsible public advocacy. Again, exercise prudence and maturity if you want people to take your petition — and the Cause — seriously.

In addition, you should consider signing and promoting other pro-South petitions you come across on the Internet. Recently, there have been numerous such petitions advocating states' rights, secession, Southern cultural/political independence, the ethnic cleansing campaign against Southerners, the removal of Confederate plaques and monuments throughout the South, and many more. Let your voice be heard.

135 *Create an Online Poll on a Southern Issue*
Contact Portrait of America's Submit a Poll site to promote Southern heritage defence, honest Southern history, state sovereignty, or Southern independence.

Utilise the Internet

136 *Print Your Own Confederate Money*
South Art has created an excellent program to print fake (for now!) Confederate money featuring a picture of General Robert E. Lee. I urge you to visit their website, save the Confederate money to your computer's desktop, and print it as needed. You should never pass information without a contact address, so consider adding the name and the Web address of your favourite Southern organisation.

137 *Create Confederate T-Shirts*
You can become a walking billboard for the South! Visit a website such as www.t-Shirts.com. Choose and design a T-shirt featuring a Southern message of your choice.

138 *Create Your Own "Confederate Message" Caps, Pens, and Bags*
Show some Southern entrepreneurial spirit. Create your own Confederate merchandise for personal use or resale. A good place to start is www.gopromos.com.

139 *Create Southern-Oriented Bumper Stickers -*
At www.victorystore.com you can design personalised bumper stickers with a message of your choice. Once you have completed your design, you can order the stickers online!

140 *Always Be on Guard*
Those working against Dixie and her values often monitor the e-mail communications on Southern-oriented list serves and websites. They are always on the prowl

for material that can be twisted or distorted to hurt and embarrass those who defend Southern heritage. Assume that whenever you write or speak someone will attempt to misquote or use your statements out of context to harm your reputation.

If you read something inappropriate or something that could be misconstrued if only bits and pieces were quoted, contact the sender and make them aware of your concerns. Remember that there are people who post false and misleading statements on Southern list serves to provoke an improper response. We are involved in a struggle where everything Southern, Confederate, or secessionist is targeted by our opponents. They will do anything to destroy this Movement because it is the last defence against government tyranny.

Conclusion

Always Be Prepared to Defend Dixie

Defending Southern heritage, history, and culture is not acceptable among the ruling classes. The Confederate flag is the worldwide symbol of resistance to oppression, authority, tyranny, and centralised government control. Do not expect any gratitude from most politicians, government bureaucrats, public school officials, large corporations, or local chambers of commerce.

Individuals and groups who make their fortunes on the backs of Southern taxpayers view those who seek to advance Southern heritage, constitutional government, and the right of secession as a threat to their revenue and, ultimately, to their existence. Southern martyr Michael

David Westerman serves as the perfect example of the antipathy felt by many toward Southerners and our Movement. He paid the ultimate cost for being proud of his Southern heritage.

I have been removed from several conference programs for no other reason than that the Third National flag of the Confederacy is displayed (on less than one percent of the pages) on my personal website. Remember, the symbols of the Confederacy generate powerful emotions — positive and negative.

Be prepared to be on the receiving end of insults and possible physical attacks. If you are not willing to face this kind of resistance to our message, you may want to shy away from open displays of Southern symbols. Many of us have paid a price for these outspoken views, as anyone who dares to resist central authority usually does. Defending freedom often carries a high cost; with this in mind, you should choose activities best suited to your personal and professional situation.

I hope and pray that all Southerners will work in unison toward a successful defence of Southern heritage and symbols, as well as a return to the limited, constitutional republic established by our Founding Fathers. My prayer is that this rebirth of liberty will take hold here in Dixie and spread across the United States like a brushfire, making the twenty-first century a time for the renewal of our freedom.

As the consummate Christian gentleman and Southern patriot, Robert E. Lee, once said, "A nation which does not remember what it was yesterday does not know where it is today." My fear is that most of us in the United States have forgotten our past and do not

Conclusion : Always Be Prepared

know where we are to-day. We have traded the freedoms gained by the Founding Fathers and defended by our Confederate ancestors for thirty pieces of silver. The attacks upon our Southern heritage and history by the sinister forces of Political Correctness are the final precondition for government tyranny and continued loss of liberty in this union. The Establishment is hell-bent upon erasing the story of the Confederates' gallant defence against Lincoln's unconstitutional war of invasion against a peaceful and independent Confederate States of America.

It is worth repeating here that only once since the American Republic was bastardised into the centralised government in Washington has any people mounted an organised, widespread resistance. The only nation to stand up to Washington and almost win was our Confederate nation; and this is why Washington feels it must destroy our history, our heritage, our spirit — and our resolve. In that vein, although we in the Southern Movement do not advocate violence or subversive action against the United States government, we do urge that Southerners band together to halt the downward slide toward oppression or, barring that, embark upon an amicable parting of the ways through democratic, legislative action — secession.

The other side has distorted, rewritten, and outright trampled our history underfoot. This also why they attempt to brainwash our children with the notion that Abraham Lincoln, the tyrant responsible for the deaths of more than 600,000 Americans (and our American Republic) was our "greatest" president. Fortunately for Dixie, there are people such as Dr. Clyde Wilson, professor of history at the University of South Carolina, and editor of *The Papers of John C. Calhoun*, who attempt to set the record straight. Read his article, *The Lincoln War Crimes Trial: A History Lesson* (available at www.lewrockwell.com/orig/wilson2.htm), and weep for what might have been had we won the War for Southern Independence.

However, as bad as things are, there is reason for encouragement. Thousands of Southerners are awakening to the realisation that the South was right and are once again taking up the banner of the Cause. (This is exactly what that the Washington/ New York political, economic, and media Establishment fears the most!) The proud, brave citizens of Dixie resisted tyranny against overwhelming odds once but were unsuccessful. Maybe next time.

Appendix A
Southern Heritage and Defence Organisations

Heritage Preservation Association
    P.O. Box 347252
    Atlanta, Georgia 30334
    Phone: 678-342-0904
    www.hpa.org

League of the South (LOS)
    P.O. Box 40910
    Tuscaloosa, Alabama 35404
    Phone: 800-888-3163
    www.dixienet.org

Sons of Confederate Veterans (SCV)
    P.O. Box 59
    Columbia, Tennessee 38402
    Phone: 800-MY-DIXIE
    www.scv.org

Southern Anti-Bigotry Coalition
    4712 Forrest Drive
    #288
    Columbia, South Carolina 29206
    Phone: 803-782-9595
    www.bigotwatch.org

Southern Heritage of the Carolinas
    P.O. Box 2935
    Concord, North Carolina 28027
    www.shccar.homestead.com

Southern Legal Resource Centre
    P.O. Box 1235
    Black Mountain, North Carolina 28711
    www.cheta.net/SLRC

United Daughters of the Confederacy (UDC)
    328 N Blvd.
    Richmond, Virginia 23220-4057
    Phone: 804-355-1636
    www.hqudc.org

Appendix B
Pro-South Websites

180 Degrees True South
    http://hammer.prohosting.com/~cward/index.html

Apologia Book Shoppe
    www.pointsouth.com/apologia/

Asset Protection and Financial Privacy Web Site Directory
    www.ronholland.com/assetprotection.htm

Asset Strategies International
    www.assetstrategies.com

Austrian & Free Market Bookstore
     www.ronholland.com/bookstores/austrian-bkstore/austrian-index.htm

Aw Shucks
     www.shucks.com

Cato Institute
     www.cato.org

Cavalier Shoppe
     www.cavaliershoppe.com

Confederate Bookstore
     www.ronholland.com/bookstores/csa-bkstore/cs-bkstore-index.htm

Congressional Report Cards
     www.vis.org/visweb/html/ratings.htm

Conservative Caucus
     www.conservativeusa.org

CSA Label Company
     www.pointsouth.com/csa-label.htm

Daily Dixie News
     www.southerncaucus.org

Dixie Calendar
     www.southerncaucus.org/calendar.htm

Appendix B : Pro-South Websites

Dixie General Store
   www.dixiegeneral.com

Dixie Web Cams
   www.southerncaucus.org/webcams.htm

Dixieland Web Ring
   www.geocities.com/bourbonstreet/2757/index.html

Fortress Dixie
   www.ronholland.com/fortressdixie2.htm

Foundation for Economic Education
   www.fee.org

Free Mississippi
   www.freemississippi.org

Freedom and Liberty Bookstore
   www.ronholland.com/bookstores/freelib-Bkstore/
   freedom-bkstore-index.htm

H. K. Edgerton Book and Video Store
   www.ronholland.com/hk2.htm

H. K. Edgerton Heritage Not Hate
   www.ronholland.com/hk1.htm

Heritage Foundation
   www.heritage.org

Heritage Preservation Association
    www.hpa.org

Home Rule for Dixie
    www.homerule-for-dixie.com

Internet-based Wealth Protection and Financial Freedom Bookstore
    www.ronholland.com/bookstores/wealth-bkstore

League of the South
    www.dixienet.org

League of the South Institute for the Study of History and Culture:
    www.dixienet.org/ls-institute/los-institute.htm

Lew Rockwell
    www.lewrockwell.com

League of the South, Missouri
    www.missourileague.com

League of the South Southern News Centre
    www.dixienet.org/dnframeset.html

Libertarian Bookstore
    www.ronholland.com/bookstores/lib-bkstore/lib-bkstore-index.html

Ludwig von Mises Institute
    www.mises.com

Appendix B : Pro-South Websites

Maurice's Bar-B-Q
www.mauricesbbq.com

Money Changer Newsletter
www.the-moneychanger.com

My Southern Party Story
www.maitreg.com/south/sp/leslie/index/asp

Olde South Limited
www.oldesouthltd.com

Petitions Online
www.petitionsonline.com

Portrait of America
www.portraitofamerica.com/html/submitapoll.cfm

Rockford Institute
www.rockfordinstitute.org

Ron Holland
www.ronholland.com

Ruffin Flag Company
www.ruffinflag.com

Sierra Times
www.sierratimes.com

Ski Dixie
www.ski-snowshoe.com

Sons of Confederate Veterans
www.scv.org

South Art
www.south-art.com

Southern Anti-Bigotry Coalition
www.bigotwatch.org

Southern Caucus
www.southerncaucus.org

Southern Heritage of the Carolinas
www.shccar.homestead.com

Southern Independence Party
www.southernindependenceparty.cc

Southern Legal Resource Centre
www.cheta.net/slrc

Southern Party
www.southernparty2000.org

Southern Party of North Carolina
www.spnc.org

Sovereign Society
www.sovereignsociety.com

United Daughters of the Confederacy
www.hqudc.org

Appendix B : Pro-South Websites

Views on the Southern Party Debacle
   www.homerule-for-dixie.com/reading/debacle.htm

Voter Information Service
   www.vis.org/visweb/html/visdb.htm

Wealth Preservation and Financial Freedom Bookstore
   www.ronholland.com/bookstores/wealth-bkstore/wealth-bkstore-index.htm

World Net Daily
   www.worldnetdaily.com

Appendix C

Pro-South Publications

Edgefield Journal
    P.O. Box 628
    Edgefield, South Carolina 29824

Sons of Confederate Veterans Magazine
    (available with SCV membership)
    P.O. Box 59
    Columbia, Tennessee 38402
    Phone: 800-380-1896
    Fax: 931-381-6712
    E-mail: exedir@scv.org

Southern Events
    P.O. Box 2517
    Selma, Alabama 36702-4057

Southern Partisan
    P.O. Box 11708
    Columbia, South Carolina 29211
    Phone: 803-254-3660

Southern Patriot
    (available with League of the South membership)
    P.O. Box 40910
    Tuscaloosa, Alabama 35404-0910
    Phone: 800-888-3163 or 205-553-0155

UDC Magazine
    (available with United Daughters of the Confederacy membership)
    328 North Boulevard
    Richmond, Virginia 23220-4057

About the Author

Ron Holland
Writer, Consultant & Patriot

Ron Holland of Asheville, North Carolina, is the editor of Dixie Daily News, a daily Internet news and political publication providing coverage of Southern history, products, heritage defense, reenactments, historical events, politics, and protests from the "Southern perspective" (http://www.southerncaucus.org).

He is by trade a financial and political writer and investment consultant and works for his own company, Holland Financial Services.

Ron is an active member in various libertarian, conservative, free-market, and heritage organizations including the Sons of Confederate Veterans, League of the

South, and Offshore Institute. He also serves on the Investment Committee of the Oxford Club and the Board of Directors for the Sovereign Society. He conducts an active schedule speaking publicly on Southern heritage and Southern Rights topics, as well as investments, economics, and finance. Ron has authored several books and written more than sixty-five print and Internet articles and reports including:

- *The Threat to the Private Pension System* (1982)

- *Numismatics — Price Appreciation/Price Collapse: It all Depends on Uncle Sam* (1984)

- *Swiss Annuities & Your Retirement Plan* (1990)

- *Global Pension Planning* (1992)

- *The Swiss Asset Protection Program* (1992)

- *The Retirement Trap* (1993)

- *The Swiss IRA Report* (1994)

- *Escape the Pension Trap* (1995)
  A 150-page explanation of the government threat to retirement plan benefits with protection strategies offered.

- *Trading with the Enemy: The Whole Story* (1997)
  A detailed explanation of the role of the Federal Reserve and the Bank for International Settle-

ments in the Nazi gold issues of World War II.

- *The Swiss Franc in the Year 2000* (1997)

- *The Swiss Gnomes Tape* (1997)
  Narrated by Louis Ruckeyser, host of "Wall Street Week," for Knowledge Products.

- *Get Ready for the Greenspan Crash* (1998)
  A warning about the 2000 and 2001 stock market mania and collapse.

- *Y2K: Will There Be An Impact on Offshore Investments?* (1999)

- *Swiss Franc: Is it Still Good as Gold?* (1999)

- *Switzerland & the Swiss Franc in the 21st Century* (2000)

Ron has also been interviewed and quoted by several national media publications and television and radio broadcasts including the *Wall Street Journal*, National Public Radio, North Carolina Public Television, C-SPAN, Cable News Network, and the Voice of America.

Most of Ron's Southern-related articles may be found in the Ron Holland Archive of the Fortress Dixie website: http://www.ronholland.com/fortressdixie2.htm. Fortress Dixie is the largest Southern website directory on the Internet, featuring more than two thousand Southern heritage, organizational, political, reenactment, product, and War for Southern Independence history sites. Listed below is cursory list of Ron's other Internet resources which may be accessed for further information.

- *The Dixie Calendar* (http://www.southerncaucus.org/calendar.htm) is a list of scheduled historical, conference, reenactment and heritage events planned for Dixie.

- *Confederate History Bookstore* (http://www.ronholland.com/fortressdixie2.htm) is a catalogue listing hundreds of War For Southern Independence books and videos available for purchase.

- *Ron Holland's Freedom Quotes* (http://www.ronholland.com/quotes/intro.htm) is a royalty-free guide to nearly one thousand historical and contemporary "politically incorrect" quotations relating to politics, freedom, economics, law, the South, and defending our liberty.

- *The Red Zone News* (http://www.redzonenews.org) is your source for non-Establishment, conservative, libertarian, and freedom news for those of us in the "Red Zone" (those counties that voted against the socialist, liberal Democrat Party agenda in the 2000 presidential election).

- *ronholland.com* (http://www.ronholland.com) provides complete non-Establishment financial, economic, global investment, and asset protection news for concerned investors of the United States who no longer trust Washington or Wall Street for financial guidance.

- *Edgerton's Heritage Not Hate Campaign* (http://www.ronholland.com/hk1.htm) allows you to follow and support black Confederate H. K. Edgerton's historic campaign to defend Southern heritage, history, and symbols.

- *Swissgnomes.com* (http://www.swissgnomes.com) provides a wealth of information about Switzerland: the Swiss franc, Swiss privacy, asset protection, and Swiss financial products and services. This website also provides links to other websites which discuss the advantages and shortcomings of Switzerland's politics, currency, etc.

Ron has used the degree he earned in Banking and Finance from the University of South Carolina to create and market over two hundred million dollars worth of financial products across the United States to conservative and libertarian Americans who believe that Big Government is a major reason for, and not the solution to, many of society's problems. His products include the first hard asset IRA in the late 1970s, first offshore Swiss Annuity IRA in Swiss francs in 1990, and the first Swiss Franc-Denominated Variable Annuity Portfolio managed by Pioneer Management Corporation in Boston. Ron's former broker-dealer, JML Swiss Investment Counselors USA, Inc., was licensed in forty-eight states and marketed over 55 million dollars in investments to clients throughout the United States from 1996 to 1999. Ron worked in bank trust services for six years prior to entering the investment business in 1982.

Mr Holland can be reached via e-mail:
    Ronholland@compuserve.com
by phone:
    Work: 1-888-550-8779
by fax:
    1-828-681-8181
by regular mail:
    Holland Financial Services
    1854 Hendersonville Road
    Box PMB6
    Asheville, NC 28803.

~Compatriots~

Left: H.K. Edgerton. Right: Ron Holland.

Heritage... Not Hate.